INFINITE CITIZEN

OF THE

SHAKING TENT

INFINITE CITIZEN

OF THE

SHAKING TENT

LIZ HOWARD

McCLELLAND & STEWART

Library and Archives of Canada Cataloguing in Publication

Howard, Liz, 1985–, author
Infinite citizen of the shaking tent / Liz Howard.

Poems.
Issued in print and electronic formats.

ISBN 978-0-7710-3836-5 (pbk.). – ISBN 978-0-7710-3837-2 (html)

I. Title.

PS8615.091154 2015   C811'.6   C2014-907898-6
                                            C2014-907899-4

Published simultaneously in the United States of America
by McClelland & Stewart, a division of Random House of Canada Limited,
a Penguin Random House Company

Library of Congress Control Number: 2014920839

Typeset in Adobe Jenson by M&S, Toronto
Printed and bound in USA

McClelland & Stewart,
a division of Random House of Canada Limited,
a Penguin Random House Company
www.penguinrandomhouse.ca

1 2 3 4 5   19 18 17 16 15

Penguin
Random
House

o ownership of the material elements of self
to toss down a dish-cloth and open a river

JOANNE ARNOTT, "dream of fine houses," *A Night for the Lady*

rendering the implicit explicit is the cognitive form of fate

PETER SLOTERDIJK, *You Must Change Your Life*

To connect is so unconquerable a citizen only a gift may vibrate.

ERÍN MOURE, "My Volition's Faint Trill," O *Cidadán*

so violent an ecstasy

PAUL LE JEUNE, *The Jesuit Relations and Allied Documents*

CONTENTS

HYPERBOREAL

OF HEREAFTER SONG

SKULLAMBIENT

HYPERBOREAL

HYPERBOREAL

TERRA NOVA, TERRAFORMED

Spent shale, thigh haptic fisher, roe, river
delta of sleep-inducing peptides abet our tent
in a deep time course, in Venus retrograde

we coalesced into the Cartesian floral pattern
of heritage where I hunt along a creek as
you pack bits of bone away within a system

of conservation the site was discovered
during construction of a new venous
highway for stars birthing themselves

out of pyroclastic dust and telepathy
in the time zone of some desperate hour
when all our exits are terraformed

Sons and daughters of the liberal arts
all my life has spurned a desire for more than
a power line of injured transistors

fetal alcohol syndrome, oil drums sunk
to the bottom of every lake, the aurora borealis
an overdose along the magnetized pole

what we are offered in lieu of a soul
another paper cut of lambent plasma
thickening the wound bed of release:

O creek, bleeding hills, census inveterate
let me sleep five more minutes just five
minutes more before we default on

eternity

NEURAL CASCADE: A CHANDELIER OF FOREST BONES

Maybe I do know you

    extensive avenue of faux moss
    vault of photochemicals upended
    on the civic leash
    mesh of resin
    a conduit
    of skulls suspended
    by reason

    a jawline fracture throttling canticles in cedar
        doubtful oxides sweating it out
        in the pineal apartment
        of our common water
        this forehead
        a portent

        for dendrites
            brain treaty
            of sap, black sap
            deep-sea atoms
            irrevocable, leaking
            what we can barely recall

        a pine marten's sacrum hanging
            its bowl of quiet from a birch
            to recognize the night inverted
            as in: I is unprovable

what is the best
        of these to be
        believed
        had you arrived
        wearing my face
        in a hail shower
        the heavens
        might've anchored

my bad shoulder
        to the floorboards
        with adrenaline, a hare gone
        to rut in the reverb of

        precognition

let me live

STANDARD TIME

In our woods: hemodynamic snow
a terrarium of lung-fed prosody
tucked inside a small body of rusted air

Our throats flecked with pyrite and broken glass
swift foxes, insulin pumps, pink cyclical rivers
know the jet stream to be a Sanguine

Melancholic in these days of warming
dark stars for lease in the divisible world
at all hours culling a distemper of infinity

Our screen test could be anaesthetic
lest my mother speak of the man who held
a gun to her head for an evening

In everything now, a gelatinous spill of best practice
could our late mouths ever know such a green word
as vertigo, vertigo, the rush of the vertical

It's ours.

Over there on the green
lawn under a sick pine
is the body of the bird
his plumage blue when
I go to look at him and
wonder if he's dead but
his chest sort of heaves
so I bend down closer
look how the breast
of the bird splits open
and a fist of maggots
spills out on the grass
a necklace of sticky
pearls in peristalsis ribbed
and shining in the July
light invertebrates that
form an anecdote before
I go back into our clapboard
house to look at the Sears
catalogue and dream
I am a girl posed into
happiness look at me
here now in this new
dress I've bought with my
own money at age twenty
in the city when the cops
question me I flash my
passport thinking of

lichen inching down
a branch of a tree over
the town river when I was
small and somewhere my
birth father is drunk and
homeless, half-mad when
the cops ask for his name
he'll say, *December*

My mother hunted moose
as a child my grandfather taught her
how to field dress a bull:
make an incision from the throat
to the pelvis
the abdominal cavity emptied
haul him up between two pines
the body inverted
antlers almost grazing
the soil
each hind limb leashed to a trunk above
to allow the flesh to cool
then she'd climb inside
the open chest
fix her toes along the ledge
of two ribs
and with a kick to the bull's left shoulder
he sent her
swinging

The total psychic economy shimmers
a latent mouthpiece of maple out in the field
anthropologically, this voice in its hollow

All night the blood moon measures the dilation
of your pupil, pinprick or dinner plate
in this plenum where our attention fails to die

A positive outcome, music in the unfinished
basement, a purple curfew for causation, the reply
a sinuous window of dried moths over the harbour

Exercise in temperament pitched back over
the clouded bathroom mirror transiting near to silver
almost female in a song of Velcro afterbirth and gravel

In our settler dreams Plexiglas teeth were stuck in the hide
of the ravine, a freeway of copper wire and sugar bush
metabolics, Copernican limbs, mercury in the water

Little silver pills tracing a path through the lake bed
of submerged logs to a trap of currents under rock
all our odd love and petrochemicals

Not otherwise
specified.

This is our welfare half
a duplex with mint green
siding shrugged between
rail yard and main street
logging trucks and trains
shake the foundation so
much I mistake them for god
forever it is winter mom
dissolves into mentholated
smoke and Coffee-Mate at
the kitchen table painting
orcas and nor'easters in burnt
umber and verdigris until
the fuel we burn for heat
dissipates I find
my brother sitting
blue-tinged in his crib
mucus freezing to his
tiny upper lip come
spring he gets up on two
feet to press his left hand
onto her canvas leaves his
mark in the sky just over
where a suggestion
of light snuck out
through the rippled
storm cloud a copper
coin shining onto where

the waters calm at a
distance from the
anonymous
shore

A WAKE

Your eyes open the night's slow static at a loss
to explain this place you've returned to from above;
cedar along a broken shore, twisting in a wake of fog.

I've lived in rooms with others, of no place and no mind
trying to bind a self inside the contagion of words while
your eyes open the night's slow static. At a loss

to understand all that I cannot say, as if you came
upon the infinite simply by thinking and it was
a shore of broken cedar twisting in a wake of fog.

If I moan from an animal throat it is in hope you
will return to me what I lost learning to speak.
Your eyes open the night's slow static at a loss

to ever know the true terminus of doubt, the limits of skin.
As long as you hold me I am doubled from without and within:
a wake of fog unbroken, a shore of twisted cedar.

I will press myself into potential, into your breath,
and maybe what was lost will return in sleep once I see
your eyes open into the night's slow static, at a loss.
Broken on a shore of cedar. We twist in a wake of fog.

DEBARKER

I just want to go back
into the bush and eat
more blueberries
growing wild as she
drops me off at the lumber
mill I'm fifteen and a janitor
cleaning out the urinals
at the debarker I find
pubic hair the lumberjacks
have left long barbs curled
to "put me in my place"
debarker: where they
keep the machine that
cuts the bark away from
the trees years ago my
blood cousin fell in
and emerged skinless
that was before this brain
sprouted from my spine
in an allegory trees
would be distributed
evenly throughout the
narrative in a gesture
of looking back over
my shoulder as mom
pulls away from the
yard I have on a hard
hat that is orange and too

big over my weird bleached
hair I have only the same
rag for the toilets as the
dishes when I look up the
sky is obscured by smoke
I can never tell what
they're burning

THINKTENT

I am my world. (The microcosm.)

– Ludwig Wittgenstein

Hospitality: the first demand
what is your name?
the city bound me so I entered

to dream a science that would name me
daughter and launch beyond
grief, the old thoracic cause

myocardium: a blood-orange foundry
handed down by the humoral
anatomists and to not be

inside my own head perpetually
not simply Wittgenstein's girl
but an infinite citizen in a shaking tent

If you are in need of an answer
consult a *jiisakiiwinini*
scientific rigour
psychoanalysis
the unconscious a construct
method amphibious
of two minds
that's the translator
her task to receive
the call that comes
down the barrel
of the future

all of us a congress
of selves a vibrational chorus
I know myself to be a guest
in your mind a grand lodge
of everything I long to know and hold
within this potlatch we call
the present
moment

If I speak of the night
speak its illicit cerebrum
of branches and back seats
speak beyond our future
a thinkable urn

my empirical training
my non-status brow ridge
indivisible and glistening

every time I tease a thread of being
from its moment in standard time

let's elevate the coordinates of distress
take it all in
I'm all in and over the limit

the limit, the eliminative, the lumens, the mens rea, the loom

to be a shopkeep in the showroom of nouns
what to purchase and what
to disavow

speak with saffron

speak of just the small bits, atomic

speak of the inevitable curve in the data

all foreclosed upon and glimmering

like a good bitch in the brine of night

I haven't nearly enough heat here

in this stakeout

the sky died and I'm its anima in the pitch thickets

I have fingers with which to squish

pin cherries and rosehips

dogwood, I have begun

to hear a rosary of pure tones, the colony

hear its call toward disorder

citizens, I have never

been dishonest in my horror

the underclass of our era

a requisite paternity test

dominus

in excelsis

Our foisted self-addendum was called against our lack
of surprise

everything that always happens
as it happens to you
in the soiled ledger of our days I know you know

we are forever evident
in our swampy coda of tending the land
is the land is its own belonging

to itself

In a laboratory of thought
lifting paper cups of black foam
up to our mouths

without cameras
everything becomes the fringe
of our interior

affect is an aid to cognition
shameless in its missionary
position of standard time

Another day unmoored
from its twin
hysterical
about music
our ontogeny
an iterative gasket
I knew it as a sphere
flinched in my portal vein
thickening and bleating and posturing
all that happened upon the digital
sidestep
the distinction
bless it
unfettered
the open stone's face

it was as if we almost knew
but then the scene changed

a false shore above the original

EPILOGUE

With light shining through my pantsuit
accidentally, I tilt
a flute of wine onto your carpet

I'm so sorry
I say
I was "lost in thought"

which means
for a brief moment
neither the flute of wine nor the carpet
existed for me
as an actionable consequence
of causality
sorry

finality is the hubris
of the new
as in act now or receive
a lesser dessert

and I'm nonetheless blind
for believing science would find us
full and laughing

bottom nature expressed as the rhythm
history of every
one

the mind in its disguise of curtains
while we wait for applause

here in my costume of forestalling
a proper exit

the account of a body in trouble could be
so beautiful

I say to you:

*excess   and its containment
is the problem space   par excellence
of late modernity*

here I am
an odd fellow

in extremis

hyperborean
all of us

only ever trying
to have a thought

SOME AMERICAS

The vertical interior of the Americas
dreamt my spine, pulling through the eye
of each vertebra a tactile thread

connecting the nape of my neck
to the foot of Tierra del Fuego
mutated derelicts of principle I am

your contagion the inconsequential air
I cannot purchase having no stake in allegory
can't climb the gate

of lucidity a raw plumage
the last vestige of reason clung to
amid a patronage of phosphorescent blue

the nuclear winter of another era
as if a punk psalm entered
my head to be unwritten

all swallows of our better misgiving
fictive tree fictive finch fictive treaty
rails and rails beyond

this pyrotechnic envelope
a cinema of self in
neurochemicals

and what now?
that I see in you no boundary
only heaven

mirror cells
in a dark marsh
make for the bridge

Wearing a hand-me-down
dress out of season in
the basement stoking the
wood stove with a can of
sunflower aerosol the wood
is wet I can't get it to light
take the can to a match
make a mini-flamethrower
that ignites the cereal box
cardboard tinder the weekly
newspaper that prints
the ministry notice about
which replanted clear-cut
will be dosed with herbicide
come spring the obituary
of old Madame C. her goitre
casting a shadow onto her
chest in the picture winners
of the fishing derby the prize
pike coming in at just over
10 pounds when my stepfather
screams from the heat grate
above my head *You dumbass!*
that'll explode in yer face
and yull be deformed n'
suicidal rest'a yer life!
crestfallen I go back
to my windowless room

open the *Inferno*'s
fire-rimmed circles
of lovable sinners

Reality appears within itself:
a bunny turns to expose a growth
irregular as an asteroid with a faint pulse

Exiting a space formerly occupied
by her right eye, there are sciences
that claim to be natural though nothing is

A false creek of straightened hair
where Galapagos is a seismic multitude
keeping time outside of traffic

Getting ready for the world atomic tour
28 neutrinos from beyond the solar system
in an ice cube a mile under the South Pole

Let the RICO of heaven come clean
the mind's eye an antique stethoscope
constantly blindsided

Fifth station of the cross, the backyard
stricken thermometers of botany
cattails and long grasses gone yellow

Either by diesel or the particular season
we find ourselves in a sonar encampment
of suffragette terns so delicate and forgetting

What little there is beyond impermanence
conspires with a half a mind on the original
to sew us closed

OF HEREAFTER SONG

... an argument for pleasure in the confusion of boundaries
and for responsibility in their construction.

DONNA HARAWAY,
A Cyborg Manifesto

the smoke that beckons
mind lapsing choleric forest
pine for coma is air treble
tremulous echo re-enter
attest circular dynamism

no nabokov reed no tidbit
no beatitude found no hyacinth

eternal the ermine and thieve reverie
eternal has ignition feathered ermine
eternal blastula even homeric for reverie
eternal thaw linger roves laced in cinder
eternal gosh angle of watered hormone
altered birth was slick and rind emergent

hung errant method
hung sky enveloped

no veridical deer no rabid name

no plenitude abound no abhorrence
no abhor
original

Is not the hybrid a melancholic? On a line between appearing + disappearing?

GAIL SCOTT,
The Obituary

CONTACT

We rested back unto the lakes and marshes
into the light dialysis of heron and arrowy
swallow with all the trees of silver tongue
gently from the melting lakes and streamlets

into the sweet radiation of the earliest flower
in the Northland intolerable toward
the red stone the stem a reed

into the puffed metastatic coal became the water

into the affirmative action embryonic mortality
of the loon summit   robin gazed

into the bigger than the big-sea-water

bioaccumulation became us Athabasca
sweet reconciliation spoke in
mercury, arsenic, lead, and cadmium
along the physiognomy of the amphibian
via which we descended

the women of bitumen looked over tailing ponds
like a cloud-rack of a tempest
rushed the pale canoes of wings and thunder
to kill the wilderness in the child
sweeping westward our remnants
sulphur infinite, sorrow extracted tuberculosis

under the jurisdiction of ravens
in the covert of pine trees

or an education by thieves in the evening.

A RUDE INSCRIPTION AT THE TOP OF HEAVEN

Hush
all the falls of pulp +
paper graveyard invertebrates
wheresoe'er the new famine wars went
before any thunder contagion muted us
in the temperature-dependent
marshlands

that opened all tributaries
of reddened mercury
when those lilies
fell me

naught a human heart nearshore the minimum
criteria

an uninterrupted silence
laid against
the fields
the fields
laid against
said DNA along the marginal pause

a disparity of garments trimmed the skin
to a threat

of arrest above
the overcrowded fog

with mosses
dioxin
so lovely

I forgot who I was

HENCEFORTH, THROUGH THE FOREST

What auspice will lend me a sacred belt?
northwind skyping
the real of consumer goods

asleep
and cumbrous
all nations in a night
terror

that's a bear
on the porch pawing
at the screen door
for meat

I wrap around this neck
a stolen show of courage
on the summit

maw plied with mosses
spotted grey and earthen
I evacuate them with red nails
before calling it a day

in a fluid movement
I remove my belt
and snap it

at the stakeholders of the commonplace
at a crucifix
at the tariff of longing
at the dawn
at my own name

heavy breathing
the hour was a body scan
and I will be as loud
as I need to

LOLing
in the middle
of mere existence
in the throes
of mystery

a thing
with claws

Fresh + simple
any possible lake
could tell a bushwhack saviour
loon's likely moved
to crown land

a place time
would inscribe
as cloudless
in the rear window
of no fiscal return

last June
in heaven
tailwaters did valley the hydro
atmospheric adverse
emergency shelters
of children taken
on advisory
boil this water
of false men
electric

among haunts
of new aquatic species
as I heard them in autumn
before the prairie also
hoofprints

half-effaced
spread

as legs in the corn
groping, lifted up
my lodges
my beaver
my own face

in the meantime
dredging every wetland
for a starry green + silent
recreational home

BIGGER THAN

Level spread
the lake my bosom
and its shadow

exaltation lifted
my liquid features
from the corroded mist

I have as much at stake
in speaking this
as the water

which also
discloses futurity
in a little black dress

for all history
awaited you
was open to you
bade you
entrance

to an unequivocal buffet
of redacted mischief
we're just friends

hanging out
in my apartment
until the world ends

and now that the world
has ended and we have not ascended
into heaven

here comes the future

let it in
let it in and let
our consumptive prom
begin

EVERY HUMAN HEART IS HUMAN

Ministry of the shaking dress
I could call this
a streamlet a better
coordinate, simply

lamprey
in the trafficking
style no matter
any purple sky
or blue vapour

tender pine
became women
working the real
number is even
higher

when I was
out already
cunting in the fields for that fallow
had escaped me

in some marsh
of insufficient housing
laughing
all the time Christ thought me
a fossil

I, Minnehaha, a small LOL
fiction antecedent
to quarry a nation

I gave you this name then said
Erase it

SKULLAMBIENT

ANARCHAEOLOGY OF LICHEN

In the towns I wear a sash monogrammed *Jacques Cartier*
and paddle through the desiccation of mute origin

if I wasn't such a *bâtarde* I'd swell dissident
and beaded aquatic, take to water

      tender stairwell of mares
      limbic foals all *miskwaa nibowin*
      red death of my arms and horses and horses

lichen for the stomachs of caribou you track me in this herd
the city now a dénouement of the assimilative purge

      symbiome: what it took for you to enter
            history, a slackened joy

John Clare and I and 37 Claires well versed in literature
each have a simulation of a raven in the crooks of our arms

      tepid swallows
         be your own antecedent
            where possible

or a coda to my bibliography of silence, a fur-lined oneirophrenia
ascetically charged moral pastures and thought systems of rivers

specious
but not for lack of wolves
or inside of wolves or beside the point of wolves
also teleology

what cache of stone flaunts umbilical sinew and lesser hides?
in a whalebone summer I'll hum "que sera, sera" on tundra

just below this earthen burial urn is our
mammalian warmth place a hand
to tend it   the
                velveteen recognition
                        slides down
                        the artifact
                                desire calcified

where all our mementos assemble subthalamic
in post-coital alluvium – all dressy – take the small bend of it

for memory for stamen for intoxicant

no sister flower could ever recover this

                        selfsame pleasure.

Amid moonscape tailings   *one brother was born*
cognition drained its basin   *on land black from the mine*

all ventricles sap and terminate   *welfare*
a girlish toss of stones into water   *sulphur*
green from copper   *apartment*

limbs angled and familial as industry   *dead and still the water*
these days without antidote   *great-grandfather worked*
tumbling into silt   *the old trap-lines*

sleek as a grey lip another cadaver lake   *into a highway with horses*
ground seepage of acids   *using dynamite to clear the shield*
hydrochloric said the railroad   *a glacier had worn*

came after the caribou or smoke   *a nest for the river*
to crack the sky open this caustic history   *his horse fell down its bank*
of moisture   *into a shattered femur*

before the caribou metabolic alleys   *nothing for the horse*
diverged   *but the dynamite*
into currents and embryos   *placed it lit*
crack the sky into a filter of words   *within its mouth*
mutagenic   *empathic demolition*

lux   *below the sole*
sucrose   *blinking traffic*
norepinephrine   *light in the centre*

whether our engine of the possible?   *of town   an elder*
asked this atomic history of silt   *diabetic amputee from*
in the watershed   *the farthest reserve*

this lift of waves   *placed his last*
recurrent   *hand on my brow*
from this shed   *called upon*
all water flows north   *Gitchi Manitou*

in a memory of sleep   *to secure my exit*
where I am four   *from poverty*
and falling through
each level of a house:

there are four corners

piles of clothes

carpets of old smoke

a staircase

mummified

placenta

brittle

slightly flaking

a soft drift

to when the cement floor signals

awakening.

FORAMEN MAGNUM

Into a concave mould of atmosphere
spilling out
of minimal consciousness

a persona or some other lineage
sedated creeks pulled under the blankets
foliage tented over clumsy mouths

a river of somnolent fauns
heady, white-tailed apnea
our sleep a fossilized memory sequence

in a crosshatch of rented weather
shake a vertebrate from its tree and dance
tramp the rafters of recollection: moss sovereign

if I allowed myself your mouth
living outside the Trans-Canada my heart
became an oil tanker fantastic

found in the forest and loosened
from its usual hunger
I'm retracing absence with a smaller claw

(in place of the third digit on the left hand)
my dull commissures pump out
something like a father in the east

what else is a river but the promise of a text
this is my delta some neural asymptote
where else could you cull such a clanging nerve?

I that I am thy.
At thy happenstance of atoms.

Were the where of my happening into happened.
But only slightly.

So many, so manlike, multiplying thusly.
Into a permanence of flux, disconcerting.

Sister.
Sister none.
Other than the keeper.
Of another heart bleeding in December.

Boys.
Some of those boys who know no boredom.
Golden, even, in the significant design.

Sing glyph.
Sing slow creep of limbs and neural tube.

Gone too far too few in fathers.
A husbandry of worms between.

There.
Over there.
The sigh almost silenced.

Thereby a maple tree.

I learned lower than blue in the public vestige where
several minute species congregated the velvet stere-
opsis when temperature loosened it was a half-uttered
sentiment in which even the tree bristled a proxy for
the sheltered evening slept its marrow in husk of
femur after walking these props for the interven-
tion of simian traffic if the cause tumbled out into
the grouping there were new expressions the future
was something liquid extended into the politic that
relegated all daughters to a camp called the sublime
where to potentiate is such a small version of the total
angle whereby your eye acquired sense to subsume
resistance like a trick of violet in cursive some minute
loops in the evening embraced the survival of a
feminine striation where the one filial strumming
did suffice phyla emergence such was our subsistence
mantra did the freakish ecology lift you disembodied
our crimes were lacquered and cured of milk the
immaculate taser shorn miracle bibliography of silence
where we entered into history a slackened joy along
the tracks of the CP Rail what is afforded by transport
sister this soil is tarred with blood rivers of remorse-
less terroir fanciful vacuum sugar apparatus in the
hindquarters of something immersive did tow the fall
of skirts over this museum into the body subterranean
became a shield of resurgent oration we could celebrate
the end of famished connection what selves said:

hey, self

are you lovely yet?

what about your sentience?

there was a filial striation

I became emergent

the tree bristled; the crimes lacquered, the liquid public, vestigial

we had a future in it

a mass was detected below the alternative space

where I surfaced and unlaced

one more mute variation

in my lung

I cut loose from the commons only to starve

did I ever have critical acumen?

did I ever bibliography with certainty?

did I ever, not in this, suffice a more barren terroir: efficiency

there was a filial striation

I became emergent.

my simian tumble, my velvet fictive, my freakish ecology

lifted

it was something only possible through a dialect

I digressed

some solar fixture before this

I assembled a trajectory

the selves

all lovely

did genuflect

PSYCHOGEOGRAPHY

From New Brunswick to Sault Ste. Marie
Bowating and northwest I came into being
with Jack pine thieves in the heronry

like Nanabozho I lost
my vision to a covenant
of ducks in vertigo
whipped a birch
to mark my name

south of the fortune
cookie factory on the
street where I lived I
lost the nerve to speak

stereotaxic
I had the stomach
of an ox
ruminative pulse
it's always one-and-the-same-thing

just north of here
down in the ravine
a friend saw a man
burying another in
the earth before dawn

one midnight I rose
to guide my hand over
the hide of a black bear
hit by a blue pickup on 129

tectonic mandibles
palpable gulls
highway silt
fetal cells
resin of a loathsome pine
these remains in the cellar
my grandmother
numbered

westward I tried it my
relations splitting cedar planks
for the sauna is about my
inheritance of base pairs
toward the substance
of some arrival

walking always this man
I call Dostoyevsky walking
his long coat and old shoes
walking who is a man who is
beautiful whose liver is diseased?

a girlhood
a head of dandelion ozone
a camp called the sublime where
several minute species
congregated
the velvet stereopsis

coyote was this young man
in the convenience store
holding a piece of raw liver
out to his friend or was this
Whitecrow in Fort Frances after the hunt?

I made love to a man lost
his rib in poison ivy there
was a collective, juvenilia and
to be a woman was to be lost
so I hugged my ribs and laughed

copper dissidence
or a fallow deer so
rabbit speak
with relevance here
and curtsey
your superlative name
– agnosia

I slept in voices of smoke
by the basement wood stove
in that house by the cemetery
to be small and dreaming parallel
to ceremony and decay

I found the body
of a Métis fur trader
in the hunt shack back there
in those woods where I guarded
him like a treasure

before I left Chapleau
for the city, which vets me
scientifically
and by its shadows
also

a false shore above the original

dearest ones please know
I'll do my best not to die young
in Toronto

HYPERBOREAL

NORTH BY SOUTH

was as if I really knew
but then the dream changed
stalactites under Mexico

become the show
ponies of our thrownness
gradually turning

into an estuary of blood and soy
bless it, unfettered
the open stone's face

there are more totem
moments where the stars
have drunk the ocean

on a self-similar
confessional flight path over
the northern hemisphere

this account of light
as an acquired characteristic
became propositional

just as every forest
would come to speak to us
as a verb

Sweet citizen, I know you
as I know myself: a fictive province
of selves within
doppler range

O body sensate
your telepathy
so impatient

soon you'll know hope
is no nutrient no last word
on forgiveness

opiate moment
unlatch the skull of a lake
from your trophy of red snow

we're in this
for the killing fields
of every biome

prosperity
a glittering dryad
felled on the horizon

If there are poems
inside the camel
brush its hump

with simple syrup
ants come and eat
the flesh away

poetry evaporates
from the wound
your boots fill

with milk in the
lecture theatre the poets
stand with their camels

we had no words
our faces became
indistinguishable

Is this an indigenous or occidental dream?
note the presence of wildlife
and anxiety about money

we stand at the lectern of origin
we stand here not only
to be counted

I felt I needed
to walk far out into
the woods through
the woods to a river
and walk upon the
waters of that river
dissolving and the silt
of me returns
to Hudson's Bay
to the Arctic Ocean, is dispersed
further into the Beaufort Sea I often
dreamt of when small
napping beside a book of maps

in another dream
it's evening
I'm to photograph
three women who face me
with their babies
bundled in their arms
poet   scientist   Anishinaabe
smile at me
and one by one
the babies
explode into flames

that same year I sat looking out
of the living room window
at a boulder across the street
a glacial erratic split into three
pieces by the growth of two birch trees

I remember when that stone was whole
my mother said behind me

this is what life does

In a tradition not quite ablated by pox
TB, and/or Christ the dreaming self
as corporeal in its endeavours
as in a waking state I go somewhere

into a kind of felicity
unforgiving

Taking our birth names we headed south
vaulting

the tractionless sphagnum
for a credit card

our only limit
will be of language

my carry-on could be your carry-on

only I am not a corpse
but a citizen

I tie a knot
around the throat of all knowledge

insist I know
where my own body was

when the whole earth retired
from intimacy

when presented with history in the form of an ellipsis
I must continue

feral, I enter
the court of words, December, December
of my mind

launch toward more than NORAD knows
of the taiga

The world is everything that is the case
it is real and it is a desert
and I'm here, hypnagogically

A fly with a metallic orange thorax on my forearm
tangents come to take you away
I can still feel you when you're gone

Synaesthesia means
A is red in my mind and the number 1 is white
inimical as the perjured self

Before the days' tarry of hooks
all memory being a kind of death
smiling and every love poem

A self-portrait of childhood
Dwight Yoakam in tan leather pants
telling me he's a thousand miles from nowhere

There's no place I wanna be
and so also
2 is red in my mind and the letter *I* is white

Pulling myself from sleep
voices from my temporal lobe or elsewhere:
Oppenheimer's air reservation

Orchids, where do they go?
the word is a purple gash I could write
a surgical line through this day

to excise the softened part
the day with its pit between my teeth
the line's quake along the surface

The sky opened onto my
simple face I'm nineteen and
begging Orion to relieve
me of an abject longing for
stasis the marshes sullied the
trenchant pleura with stuccoed
purpose beseeched me in the
flagrant errors of any small
girl there is the stuff of
fables whether false or
guileless in speaking of what
happens my mother combing
through trash at the landfill
I'm twelve out among the
ravens and black bears in an
air of death I sit in the back of
the flatbed truck knees to my
chest reciting, *Tomorrow and
tomorrow and tomorrow* from
the entrance the gatekeeper
smiles without teeth and winks
at me then it's fifteen years
later I sit in the innocuous
green of late summer I who
unfolds in full view for no one
in particular I rest one foot on
the curb the other on the roof
of the world's mouth so much

that is beyond me high beams
on the dividing line of
the highway I take my
galvanic bath outdoors to
repair any derelict vowel
if even your forests abandon
the crucible of self and grow
weary into a climax of fur
Manitouwadge, Manitoba,
Manitoulin in situ it is neither
I nor the white of it nor you
who are yellow and black
and gold Orion we all
should have been born on a Tuesday

These canticles of cedar burn skyward
out from the woods where blood has rusted snow
our fierce theatre split between two worlds
liberal arts by proxy flank every pole

Our basement a psychic economy
of static fog and what we cannot know
the odd love we burn for heat dissipates
and each spine sprouts a new-found yellow smoke

Any limb could learn its place in the pines
the fact of standard time is illicit
the broken flight of a bird half-shining
measured by the extent of a street light

No perfect confidence in being born
still we dream of Tierra del Fuego

REVENANT: MISREMEMBERED

In our old apartment
epiphytes and dark stars
left behind and inside me
a paper cut of lost sleep

One afternoon with Copernicus
and I've learned to doubt with my eyes open
the table is mentholated water
my shoulder pulled away from the gesture

A ledge of toes under each dress
my lips were kiss-chapped and spectral
a necklace of money I flash at the modus of power
resurrected in a need for extension

Habitually, honey
poured from the cinema of our better misgivings

Adrenaline
Tetra Pak jets of anaesthetic
a failure in Latin
fetal oil drums cut from
the curfew of dilated freeways
or the terminus of animal doubt

A mucosal crib of unknown distance
the sky a barb of blue wanting
everything abdominal and yet to be emptied
in a daffodil chorus of posthumous laughter
this clapboard passport
where Wordsworth is a doll

The unsubstantial structure melts the embryonic
psalms of heaven, all lushly punk and pyrotechnic

Hills of pseudoephedrine and lavender
  you fell away

through the abortive canopy overhead
  ochred the earth

with red needles I will ask you again
  where is my good

gloss? under the pulpit, ammonia and wine
  I required a field

guide to persuade the hours into use
  but found only

scraps of old paper, receipts, transfers
  scrawled with

illegible coordinates I had only my legs inside
  some red shredded

tights as I went headlong down the ravine
  my collar bone

flexed its impression into the soil
  what is left

to be said through the gap under
  the door

I can't tell you how many times
    I've tried

to find this easy and just close
    my eyes

to become one of those women
    who can wreck

the infinite as if I ever knew a swallow
    to be more than

its significant derivative in my dream
    Erín Moure told me

Don't let the oligarch of your cup get into
    the network

swimming a heavy-handed reflexive crush
    my forebrain

a lesser charge I radiate some stumbling argument
    with the fog

concomitant and coming in droves our winters
    a modern retelling

of forced labour selling milk in the woods
    sisters I continue

to mop in the direction
    of pleasure

RING SAMPLE: ADDENDUM

You bleed a moss creek, I'll halve a bone fisher
unprovable in the hail, I invert our quiet atoms
infinity rushes our small bodies into distemper
our questions spill out onto the green money, your passport

swinging from the incision along my child's throat
a song of copper wire and submerged currents
come spring we'll burn the anonymous kitchen into verdigris
a static fog inside the animal I am, and doubled

out from the machine that cuts the skin away from belief
I knew it as a dream flinched in my potlatch another animus
rhythm history expressed as the bottom nature of every one
our mashes darkest, our lucidity an unwritten thread

sinners, lovable, fallen wet in the tinder
a delicate sonar with our pulse on the original

BINGO RIOT

Coterie of the senseless
I will not refuse the moons
you show me

caught in the gutter water
body glitter
hypodermic, a pocked

nickel from the '70s
your jean waist is high
higher than your actual waist

here's the horizon coming into view
a spackling of misremembered stars
that misremembers you

as someone from high school
in a town you haven't met
the light breaks red orange

gorgeous across the symmetry
of your face under the viaduct
I am laughing

at the perfect nothing I find
in my hand my father is missing
the future is approaching

on horseback
clopping metrical fits along
Lake Superior's shore

the night rears up from under
this lost fur inversion
modernity is so destabilizing

as is the architecture of any bird's
wing the carpals the metacarpals
of my hand the fingers phalanges

the rivers of northern Ontario
all at length elaborate the dawn
as our baroque moment qua

the gorgeous brokenness the viaduct
is a glitter of lacklace
you say you have a culvert to your name

its brackish echoes fracture into
the reeds the diesel the fertilized
emblem of a culture disabused

to abandon the regular stars that
mark your arrival
in the community shelter the orange

is porous a kind of dawn seeping into
the storage space where
we have accounted for our nouns

the coterie is split along a conjugal axis
these urban foxes bury
our wisdom teeth by the river

the bingo of happenstance has
already started but we have
no amulets for trust

your jeans are high above
my face I don't know what to say
the feeling erases me

the city the township the home
range displaced the cattle the caribou
the day itself displaced sea swell

and fenestrae, the unintelligible
diction we are wont to swallow
across transatlantic silicon

hear your clinic, hear it clear
what hand over my plush-covered gills won't sing?
forged from Algoma steel

receive me caught in mayflies
a verdant symptom through
the porch screen of you

in this sinkhole of time called the present
exquisite kinship we coddle our knees
against the stolen furniture

we simply tumble down
the rote division
of light

ANISHINAABEMOWIN GLOSSARY

Jiisakiiwinini: spiritual healer who conducts the Shaking Tent rite wherein spirits are consulted to obtain beyond human knowledge

miskwaa: red

nibowin: death

Gitchi Manitou: Great Spirit

Bowating: original name for Sault Ste. Marie, Ontario

Nanabozho: trickster figure and cultural hero

Henry Wadsworth Longfellow's 1855 epic *The Song of Hiawatha* appropri-
ated and confused Anishinaabe history and mythology and inserted/
naturalized a colonial presence within Anishinaabe cosmology. It is a
textual assimilation of Indigenous rhythmic oration into a bombastic
trochaic tetrameter, itself borrowed from the Finnish national epic
Kalevala. Minnehaha, a creation of Longfellow, was the spouse of
Hiawatha, whose death set the stage for the reception of settler influence
later in the poem. "OF HEREAFTER SONG" is something of a trans-
lational détournement of *The Song of Hiawatha*, an intertextual recombi-
nation, filtered through the sited embodiment of myself and subsequent
readerly selves; it engages the systemic tentacles of assimilation as they
unfurl within and possibly enclose the contemporary New World.
Words and phrases from Longfellow's epic are sampled and remixed. As
I am both settler and Indigenous, the text may contain the sweet horrors
of my diary, a girlish self-narrative that arose from the once-irreconcilable.
Language is also thrifted from ecological reports on the Lake Superior
region, in which the original text is set, and sociological reports regard-
ing the injustices lived by many Indigenous women, men, and two-spirit
persons. These injustices are an inevitable extension of the ideologies
inscribed in Longfellow's poem. "OF HERE" is a linguistic performance
that seeks to display/acknowledge its own implication in the effects of

assimilation while simultaneously revealing those ideologies that underpin the assimilative program as it operates to this day.

"Ring Sample: Addendum" is a recombinative sonnet that constitutes a dendrochronology of language pulled from the first 14 poems of the book. The preceding "Revenant" poems constitute an earlier foray into this strategy and linger here as a necessary haunting.

ACKNOWLEDGEMENTS

The writing of this work was supported by a Toronto Arts Council Writers Grant and a Social Sciences and Humanities Research Council Joseph-Armand Bombardier Canada Graduate Research Scholarship.

Previous iterations of several poems appeared in *The Capilano Review*, *ditch*, *The Puritan*, *The Rusty Toque*, in the anthology *Toward. Some. Air.* (Banff Centre Press), and the chapbook *Skullambient* (Ferno House Press). Special thanks to the editors of these publications: Jenny Penberthy, Kathryn Mockler, Amy De'Ath and Fred Wah, and Mat Laporte and Spencer Gordon.

Thanks to my editor Ken Babstock for his fierce intelligence and reassurance.

Profound thanks to Dionne Brand for her keen attention to my work, to Margaret Christakos for deft guidance and encouragement, to Lisa Robertson for her mentorship and generosity, and to Erín Moure for her continuing support.

Thanks to the excellent team at M&S, especially Anita Chong and Ellen Seligman.

I have been supported by many friends, colleagues, and family throughout the writing of this book. Simply listing their names here does little justice toward the gratitude I have for them or for the measure of their influence and love. Infinite thanks to: my partner, David Whitton; my poetic godmother, Lynn McClory; fellow Influencers Sonja Greckol, Ralph Kolewe, Joan Guenther, and Eric Foley; Kerri Scheer, Richie Stevens, Cara Chellew, and Jaime Whitecrow for unwavering friendship; and the following fellow workshoppers, reading hosts, and poets: John Bell, Sean Braune, Natalie Marie Helberg, Shannon Maguire, Jimmy McInnes, Jay and Hazel Millar, Edward Nixon, Ariana Reines, Meaghan Strimas, Fenn Stewart, Jess Taylor, and many, many others. Thanks to my employer, Professor Lynn Hasher, and the members of the Aging and Cognition Lab. Thanks to my parents, Tamara and Sylvain Rousseau, the Howard family, my grandmother Betty Ann Turcotte, and my brothers, Jameson and Nelson.

Finally, a big thanks to you the reader. *Chi-miigwetch. Merci.*